# Happens to Them?

what every **parent** needs to know
about **estate planning**

## Chuck Roulet, J.D.

WORD ASSOCIATION PUBLISHERS
www.wordassociation.com
1.800.827.7903

ISBN: 978-1-59571-988-1

*Designed and published by*
Word Association Publishers
205 Fifth Avenue
Tarentum, Pennsylvania 15084

www.wordassociation.com
1.800.827.7903

# Table of Contents

# About The Author

Minnesota will, trust and estate planning attorney Chuck Roulet has devoted his career to helping clients protect what matters most to them through comprehensive estate, asset protection, and business planning.

Chuck is a frequent lecturer, presenting both locally and nationally on estate planning and business law. Chuck is also the recipient of the CALI Award for Excellence in Estates and Trusts.

Chuck resides in Minneapolis, Minnesota with his wife and two children.

For more information, please visit www.RouletLaw.com

# Disclaimer

You weren't expecting to read a book by a lawyer and not have some sort of disclaimer, were you?

**Disclaimer:** This work is not intended to be either legal or ethical advice. NEITHER TRANSMISSION NOR RECEIPT OF THESE MATERIALS CREATES AN ATTORNEY-CLIENT RELATIONSHIP BETWEEN YOU AND THE AUTHOR OR PUBLISHER. This book provides information about the law. But, legal information is not the same as legal advice -- the application of law to an individual's specific circumstances. In addition, federal, state or local tax law changes, variations or procedural rules may have a material impact on the general information provided by the author and the strategies outlined in this book may not be suitable for every individual. Effort has been made to assure that the information contained in this book is accurate and useful. However, it is recommended that you consult a lawyer and/or tax professional if you want assurance that the information, and your interpretation of it, is appropriate to your particular situation.

The publisher and author make no representations or warranties with respect to the accuracy or completeness of the contents of this work and specifically disclaim all warranties, including, without limitation, warranties of fitness for a particular purpose.

# Introduction

Do you know what would happen to your kids in the event anything ever happened to you?

When I speak to a group, I often ask this question of the audience and then ask for a show of hands of those who think they know the answer. As the hands go up, I then go through and ask each of them a series of follow up questions about the plan in place for their kids. Usually, a majority of the parents have made at least one of the mistakes I will talk about in Chapter 1 of this book. Others will have made one or more of the mistakes I will discuss in Chapter 3. As I work through the room with the follow-up questions, most parents are laughing as they realize not a single hand remains up. I do this to make the point that most parents simply don't know what they don't know when it comes to protecting their kids in the event anything were to happen to them.

Even parents who have previously worked with an attorney are often surprised to find out that they do not *really* know what would happen to their kids, that many of their plans would not protect their children or that the money they leave them might not make their kids' future as financially secure as they would want.

Can you answer these questions?

1. In the event anything ever happened to you, do you know who would raise your children and with what values?

2. Do you know who would manage their money and when they would get it?

3. Do you know how to protect what you've left for them from potential creditors or in the event they ever get divorced?

4. Have you left enough for your kids?

5. Was your current estate plan *really* written for someone in their sixties, and not designed to protect you, your family, your goals, or your values?

6. Do you know you need to do something, but don't know how to proceed, what questions to ask or who you can trust to protect what matters most to you?

I've written this book to help you answer these questions. That's because I'm not just an attorney, I'm also a dad.

As I sat holding my newborn daughter for the first time, I knew my life had changed forever. I was a dad. I was at once exhilarated, exhausted, excited and, frankly, a little scared. I felt the awesome responsibility of protecting, providing for and guiding my child. I knew my actions would ripple through generations.

I'd had my fair share of responsibility prior to becoming a dad. I had worked as a legislative assistant at one of the largest law firms in the world in the heart of Washington, DC. I spent my days on the phone with the White House and with the staffs of prominent members of Congress, and provided research assistance to lawyers who argued before the United States Supreme Court. I had represented a German bank, sold publicly-traded companies, moved assets around the globe and counseled clients twice my age on the protection of their life savings. Yet, none of it prepared me for the awesome responsibility of being a parent.

I will never forget putting my daughter in her car seat for the first time as we prepared to leave from the hospital and thinking to myself, "They're really just going to let us leave with her?!" Normally possessed of a lead foot, I found myself with a new appreciation for the people who drive precisely 55 mph in the right hand lane as we drove home from the hospital.

At work, I started asking questions as a dad, and not just as an attorney. I was asking all of the questions above and a whole lot more. Surprisingly, I didn't like the answers I was given. I realized that many of the estate plans that were being created for clients were based off of plans used for people in their sixties and then just re-used for clients with minor children. As such, they were likely to fail when the family needed them most.

It is my goal with this book to help answer the questions you may have about how to protect your children in the event anything ever happened to you. I have also included the "should ask questions" – the questions that I as an attorney know that you should be asking but that you may not know about yet. I want to share with you some of the secrets I've learned in my years of experience as an attorney who is also a dad. I want to help you put your own plan in place that will protect your children in the way that you want, how you want, and ensure that they are raised with the values that are most important to you, while providing them with a lifetime of support and guidance.

# CHAPTER 1

# Do You Know What Would Happen To Your Children If Something Ever Happened To You?

The title of this chapter asks a difficult and uncomfortable question. Maybe you've thought about it. Maybe you haven't. Do you know what would happen to your children in the event something ever happened to you? As a parent, if you don't know the answer to that question with absolute certainty, then you owe it to your kids to give it some serious thought and then get a written plan in place to protect them.

The experience of one family illustrates what could happen to your kids if something ever happened to you. On July 31, 2006, a California family – Melanie and Casey Barber and their three sons, ages eight, five and three – were involved in a car accident. A tire separated and their van rolled on the highway. Melanie and Casey died. Their three sons survived.

Since Melanie and Casey did not have a written document in place naming guardians for their kids, the decision fell to a judge. The boys spent some time in foster care since the judge needed time to review the options before appointing a long-term guardian. Then they went to stay with one of their aunts – who allegedly kept them from seeing some of the other family members – while the extended family went to court to fight over who would raise them.

In the subsequent proceedings, over 1,000 pages of court documents were filed, nine lawyers were involved and tens of thousands of dollars were spent deciding who the guardian of the boys should be. Court documents reflect that the Barbers had talked about naming guardians for their three sons, but since nothing was in writing, a judge had to decide.

In a separate lawsuit, a jury awarded the boys $14.4 million in a wrongful-death suit against a car dealership that did work on the van and another $8.3 million settlement was reached with others who had done work on the van. When all was said and done, a judge decided who would raise the boys, who would manage their money and when they would receive it. Was it what Melanie and Casey would have wanted for them?

Parents often make the mistake of thinking that because they discussed who they would want as the guardians of their children with the potential guardian and/or other friends and family, those people would automatically be appointed. As illustrated in the Barber case, in the absence of a written nomination, properly executed by you, a judge would have to decide who to name as the guardian of your children.

# Short-term Guardians and Your Family Emergency Response Plan

You may be surprised to learn that your kids could end up in foster care in the event of an emergency. However, as the Barber family story illustrates, foster care could be the first place your children go in an emergency, while a judge decides what to do with them.

I was once asked to speak to parents at a daycare center. During the presentation, the executive director reinforced the need for short-term guardians to the parents in attendance. She shared that in the event that parents were more than two hours late to pick up their kids, could not be reached, and did not have short-term guardians on file as prescribed by state law, their instructions were to contact child protective services (foster care) to come pick up the kids.

My sister-in-law used to work in a foster care center. She shared the story of a little girl who was taken into foster care. Her parents were involved in a bitter divorce and were arguing in court. The judge got angry and ordered the little girl into foster care. She spent 48 hours there until her grandmother – who was ready, willing and able to care for her – fought to get the right to care for her pending the finalization of the divorce proceedings.

A few years ago, I was invited to speak at a parents' group about what parents need to know to protect their kids. When I finished the section on short-term guardians and a written family emergency response plan, a woman in the back of the room raised her hand. She shared with the group that she and her husband were foster parents and were often called upon to provide foster care for kids whose parents were not able to take care of them.

While the list of reasons included the things one might normally associate with foster care, such as substance abuse and neglect, she shared that over the years they had a number of kids come to them from stable families whose parents had been involved in accidents and the kids had been placed with them while a judge decided who among the family should have them.

If anything happened where you could not provide care for your children, there is the possibility that your children would be placed with child protective services (foster care) until you either get well enough to give alternative instructions or until a judge determines who should care for your children. Child protective services would most likely attempt to find a relative to care for your children. However, they may remain in foster care until family members are identified and selected. The person who is selected might not be the person who you would have chosen. For example, your kids could go to your brother-in-law who only sees them once a year for the holidays, and not with your best friend who sees them every week.

That is why it is important to get a written family emergency response plan in place for your family that includes naming short-term guardians (what I also refer to as emergency first responders) who are authorized to provide immediate care for your children. When preparing a family emergency response plan, you name who you would want as your short-term guardians in the event of an emergency. We usually suggest friends or family who the kids know and are comfortable with. We also recommend including people who live within twenty minutes or less of you so that they can respond quickly, if needed.

It is important to provide your short-term guardians with a power of attorney so they would have the authority to make necessary decisions. We also suggest that your short-term guardians be given medical power of attorney so that they are able to make medical decisions for your kids if necessary due to federal HIPAA laws. There will be more on this in upcoming chapters.

We recommend that copies of your paperwork be given to your short-term guardians as well as daycare facilities, schools and extracurricular activities. That way, in an emergency your short-term guardians would be able to pick up your kids without having to first go home and find their copy of the paperwork. We also suggest having emergency ID cards in your wallets informing any emergency personnel that you have minor children and who to contact in an emergency. In our practice, we prepare these cards for our clients and include our contact information in case there are questions.

It is important to note that even if you previously worked with an attorney to prepare an estate plan for your family, you may not have a family emergency response plan in place. In fact, surprisingly, the majority of parents I encounter who had their estate plan prepared by someone else do not have a family emergency response plan included as part of their estate plan. If you have an estate plan already in place, this important step may have been overlooked and it would be worth having your plan reviewed. My home state of Minnesota has two specific statutes stating what is required to authorize short-term guardians. Your state and its laws may be different, so you should consult with an experienced attorney to get your written family emergency response plan in place.

# CHAPTER 2

# You Will Never Be Replaced: Protecting Your Children In The Event Something Ever Happened To You

In the last chapter, we discussed what would happen to your children in the short-term in the event something ever happened to you. In this chapter, we will discuss what would happen to your children in the long-term.

If something were to happen to you, unless you a have a written document complying with your state laws stating your choice of long-term guardians for your children, a judge would decide who will raise them. A judge, despite his or her best efforts, simply does not have all the information you do about who would be the best choice to raise your kids. With limited time and limited information, the judge would be forced to make a decision impacting the lives of your children, may use criteria that you would not have used in making that decision and may end up appointing someone you would not have wanted. Also, your family could end up fighting over who should raise your kids – adding more stress, anxiety and expense to their and your children's lives.

For example, a judge could be presented with two options for whom to appoint as guardian of your kids. Let's say the first option is your 25-year-old sister, who just completed graduate school and is living in an apartment. She is starting a new career and is enjoying her single lifestyle. The second option is your brother-in-law and his wife, who are financially secure, live in a nice home close to where you and your children live and have two young children of their own.

If you were this judge, which guardian would you place your children with? I think the answer is pretty clear that most judges would choose your brother-in-law and his wife. But, what if you did not approve of the way your brother-in-law and his wife were raising their own kids and would not want your kids raised that way? What if you knew that your younger sister would step up and really be the best choice for your kids – raising them in the way you would want and with the values that are most important to you? In the absence of written instructions to the contrary, it is highly likely that the guardian of your kids would be someone that you would not have wanted.

The best way to help ensure that your kids would be raised by who you want, how you want and with the values that are most important to you is to make sure you get it in writing. You never want to leave the decision of who would raise your kids to a judge. You also never want to put your family in the position of fighting over who would raise them and how.

In the event that something ever happened to you, you would never be replaced in the lives of your children. However, with your advance planning, your children would be surrounded by the love and guidance they need, and in the best possible position to maximize who they are and their unique talents and gifts. Taking the time to choose your children's guardian based on the criteria most important to you is better than leaving it up to a judge to decide. It would also be easier on your family and much better for your kids.

# CHAPTER 3

# Mistakes Parents Make When Naming Guardians For Their Children

Over the years, I have seen parents make numerous mistakes when it comes to naming guardians for their children, even if they previously worked with an attorney. That is because they may not have received the guidance they needed to avoid these simple and common mistakes.

## Mistake #1:
## Failing to exclude anyone who you would not want or who might challenge your wishes.

For some of my clients, there is at least one person in their family who they would not want to be the guardian of their children and/or that they think might possibly challenge who they have nominated as a guardian.

If you have a situation like that, consider a written exclusion of guardian. This is a very simple document that states that in the event the person or people listed ever challenge who you have appointed as a potential guardian, you want it known that you would not want them to be the guardian of your children. You do not have to give a reason for excluding them and you can even request that the document remain private, only becoming public in the event a listed person were to actually challenge your nomination.

## Mistake #2:
## Failing to include a list of family and friends who you would want to have involved in the lives of your children.

A now famous case in Pennsylvania illustrates why you need to make a list of the people who you would want to continue being involved in your children's lives in the event something ever happened to you. A mother with a young son was dying of cancer. Her mom helped take care of the son almost every day during the last couple years of the young woman's life. The grandma and grandson had a very close relationship. After the boy's mom died, his dad refused to let his grandma spend any more time with him. Ultimately, the Supreme Court of Pennsylvania allowed the grandmother to spend one weekend per month and one week per summer with her grandson.

This case illustrates the potential for guardians you name to restrict your children's access to other loved ones. If you have people who you definitely want involved in your children's lives, make sure you name them in writing as part of your overall estate plan.

# Mistake #3:
# Naming a couple to act as your children's guardians.

You are probably asking yourself right now, how can naming a couple to act as my children's potential guardians be a mistake? It is a mistake if you are not completely comfortable with both of the people you name to raise your children on their own.

Here is the example I most often see: You name a sibling and the sibling's spouse as guardians. For illustration purposes, we'll assume the couple is your sister and her husband. You have now named both of them. In the event the couple were to get divorced, you have now left the decision of who should be the children's guardian up to them, their attorneys and the divorce court. Alternatively, imagine the consequences if something were to happen to your sister. Because your brother-in-law was named as co-guardian, he would continue in that capacity. If you are comfortable with your brother-in-law ever being the sole guardian of your children, then naming the couple to act as guardian is OK. However, if you would *not* want your brother-in-law to act alone as guardian, then consider naming *just* your sister.

# Mistake #4:
# Failing to name alternatives in case your first choice is unable to act as your guardian.

Following the example in mistake #3, what if you named your sister only and, when called upon, she had an event in her life that would make it difficult, if not impossible, for her to act as guardian? Or, what if your sister had already predeceased you? In the absence of a written alternative, you have left the decision of who should be the guardian of your children to a judge. If possible, you should name at least one alternative guardian in the event your first choice is unable to act for you.

## Mistake #5:
## Making the financial resources of a potential guardian the primary consideration.

As part of the estate planning process, you should be sure to leave enough money for your kids in the event anything ever happened to you, either through savings or life insurance. That way, you are free to choose the guardians you really want for your kids – the ones who would be best able to nourish your children's emotional, spiritual and physical wellbeing – without making finances the primary consideration for your choice. While the financial resources of a potential guardian are an important consideration in your decision, they should not be the primary deciding factor.

## Mistake #6:
## Failing to name someone to manage the money you leave for your children.

You should select someone who can responsibly manage the money you leave for your children until they are old enough to receive and manage it themselves. If you fail to specify who should manage the money and when your children should receive it, a judge will decide who manages the money, how it is managed and most likely allow the children to receive it outright and unprotected at age 18. The person you select to manage their money can be the same person you name as your guardian – but it doesn't have to be. Also, you should specify how the money you leave for your children is to be managed and when they should get it. You should also make sure that the money is properly protected from creditors, predators and failed marriages. This will be covered in later chapters.

## Mistake #7:
## Failing to leave written instructions for your guardians.

You should leave detailed, written instructions for your guardians letting them know what school the kids are in, what activities you would like them to continue being involved with, what belief system and church or faith community they have been involved in, your thoughts on discipline, any important medical conditions, as well as other important details. Stop for a moment and think about all of the little details of your children's day-to-day activities. It is important that you make sure that a potential guardian would have that valuable information.

## Mistake #8:
## Failing to give your guardians the legal authority and instructions they need to make medical decisions for your children.

In the event your guardians ever needed to make medical decisions for your children, they would need the legal authority to do so. Thanks to the federal law known as the Health Insurance Portability and Accountability Act or "HIPAA," our medical information is better protected than ever before. However, the law makes it more difficult for family and friends to help with medical decisions in an emergency.

HIPAA requires that third parties have written authorization in order to receive medical information. That means that in order for your short-term guardians to receive the information they would need to make an informed medical decision about the care and treatment of your children, they would need to be authorized by you in writing.

Without written authorization from you, it is possible that a potential guardian would need to seek approval from a judge to help your children in a medical emergency, even if they have been named by you as the short-term guardian. The reason for this is that HIPAA and its protections of medical records is a federal law, but laws concerning short-term guardians are state laws.

To ensure that the short-term guardians of our clients' children would always be able to make decisions for their kids if they ever needed to, we prepare a separate medical power of attorney for each of their children giving potential guardians HIPAA authority. It is critical that your short-term guardians have this written authorization in advance so that in an emergency they can step in and make decisions for your children without the delay and expense of seeking court approval first.

I also advise all of my clients to list any specific medical conditions their children have, along with any instructions they have for the care of their children. Your written instructions will help guide a potential guardian in the event they need to make important medical decisions for your children.

# Mistake #9:
# Taking tomorrow for granted.

We all assume tomorrow is a given. If you want to make sure that in the event something ever happened to you that your children would be raised by who you want, how you want, and with the values and guidance most important to you, then you need to get it in writing in a manner that complies with your state laws.

# CHAPTER 4

# You Don't *Need* An Estate Plan (As Long As You Like The One The State Has For You And Your Family)

If you fail to prepare a written estate plan, the state you live in has one for you. All states have laws that probate court judges follow for those who do not have a written estate plan in place. This default estate plan for you and your family will determine who is in charge of your assets and where they will go upon your passing. In my experience, once people understand the state's plan for their family and their assets, they make sure to get a written estate plan in place.

In the event you were to pass away without a written estate plan, a situation known as "intestate," someone would need the legal authority to sign the paperwork to transfer ownership of your assets. Your home, bank accounts, life insurance, retirement accounts, vehicles, etc., may require someone with the legal authority to sign the paperwork necessary to transfer ownership of that asset and a probate court would appoint that person. The person who gets appointed is known as the personal representative.

**Selecting the Personal Representative.** Anyone with an interest in your estate can petition to be the personal representative, and "interest in your estate" is a broad term. That means a family member, any beneficiary, the bank where you have your checking and savings accounts, your mortgage company and insurance company could all petition. In the event more than one person petitions to become your personal representative, the court will hold a hearing to determine who it should be, usually based on an order of priority established in state law. The take away for you is that someone other than the one you would want or think would be your personal representative could end up being appointed. Also, families frequently fight over who should become the personal representative because this person will control your estate for the duration of the probate process.

**Managing the Estate Assets.** Once the personal representative has been appointed, their job is to collect all of the assets, pay all of the bills and account for everything in the estate. Once that is done, they distribute the assets to the beneficiaries of the estate as determined by the probate court.

**The Court determines who the beneficiaries are and when they receive the assets.** Without a written estate plan, the beneficiaries of your estate will be determined by the probate court according to state law. That means it is entirely possible that your assets could go to people you would not even want – and in ways you would not want. For example, if you have minor children, the court will determine who manages the money you leave for your children and how it will be managed. Unfortunately, with the state's default plan for your family your children will likely get their inheritance outright and unprotected at the age of 18. Do you want your children to get a significant amount of money unprotected and at the age of 18? What if you have children from a previous marriage? How would you want your estate split between your current spouse and all of your children? In the absence of a written plan, the court will decide for you, and it may not be what you would have chosen.

**Probate is expensive.** Probate is an expensive process. Here is a list of some of the expenses involved with probate:

Court Costs. Court costs run anywhere from a few hundred dollars to thousands of dollars.

Personal Representative Fees. The personal representative needs to be paid for their services. In some states, the personal representative is given a fixed percentage of the estate while in others they receive a "reasonable fee." A personal representative can also petition for "extraordinary fees."

Attorney's Fees. The attorney who works with the personal representative also needs to be paid. Like the personal representative, some states provide for a fixed percentage of the estate for attorney's fees while others provide for a "reasonable fee." The attorney may also petition for "extraordinary fees."

Accounting Fees. There are also accounting fees. A small estate with a lot of assets may actually require more accounting work, and higher fees, than a larger estate with fewer assets. If your estate is taxable at your death, at either the state or federal level, there will be additional accounting fees to prepare and file estate tax returns.

Bond Fees. If you do not have a written will that waives the requirement of a bond, your personal representative may need to post a bond with the probate court. (Note that even if you have a will that waives the requirement of a bond, if you have minor children the probate court may still require one from the personal representative.)

Appraisal Fees. The values of real estate and personal property (jewelry, antiques, boats, cars, etc.) at the date of death will need to be determined. Also, if you own a business, a business valuation will need to be done. These fees can range from a few hundred to thousands of dollars.

Miscellaneous Fees. These fees include storage and shipping of property and can add up quickly.

Many estimates put the cost of probate at 2%-5% or more of your gross estate, depending on the state. Stop for a moment and add up the equity in your home and any other real property you may own, the value of your retirement accounts, life insurance, cars, antiques, artwork, bank accounts and so forth, and then multiply that by 2%-5%. If your total estate was approximately $1 million, probate could cost your family as much as $20,000-$50,000 or more, depending on factors such as which state you live in, the size of your estate and whether there are any disputes against the estate.

**Probate takes time.** Probate also takes time. Depending on your home state, probate can take anywhere from three to six months to several years. In my home state of Minnesota, we estimate probate to take 12-16 months. If you own a small business or have minor children, it can take two years or more. In fact, I recently met with a client who shared that her brother passed away four years ago and they are still dealing with probate. She also let me know – and it's something I hear from every client who has ever experienced probate firsthand – that they wanted to do "whatever we can to make sure our kids do not have to go through the probate process!" This holds true for even the most experienced clients: I recently had a retired probate court clerk and her husband meet with me who mentioned that they wanted to do whatever it took so that their family would not have to go through the probate process. As you'll see in an upcoming chapter, that is definitely possible with proper planning.

## Probate is public. Ever wonder why the press is able to comment on the details of the wills of Jackie Kennedy, John Lennon and other famous people?

For example, just how does *Fortune* magazine know that Jackie Kennedy gave one of her friends a Greek alabaster head of a woman? How does the *New York Times* know that J.P. Morgan bequeathed a year's salary to each of his employees upon his passing? It's because wills are public. Anybody can go down to the courthouse and pull a probate record. That means they know how large your estate is, who you owe, what you have, who is getting what, and how much and when, because it is all laid out in the probate records. Because probate records are public, many unsavory people troll the probate filings. As a result, we are seeing identity theft and scams aimed at beneficiaries. After my grandmother passed away, we found several fraudulent credit cards in her name as a result of public information in the probate filings.

# Joint ownership with a spouse does not eliminate probate.

When I discuss probate in my seminars, I frequently get a variation of the following question: "My wife and I own everything jointly. If I die first, my spouse will get everything without probate. If my spouse dies first, I will get everything without probate. So why do we need an estate plan to avoid probate, since it looks like we will avoid it anyway, right?"

Wrong. If you die, your spouse will indeed own all of your jointly owned property without probate. If your spouse dies first, you will indeed own all of your jointly owned property without probate. The problem is when the last of you dies, there will be a probate. Owning everything jointly does not avoid probate, it just puts it off until the last of you passes away. And in the event you do not own everything jointly (such as a bank account, small business, hunting land or other piece of real property), your family may have to go through the probate process twice: once upon your passing and again upon the passing of your spouse. That means double the time, expense and aggravation of probate for your family. And as you'll discover in other chapters, without an estate plan you may miss the opportunity to lock in certain protections that shield your estate from creditors and estate taxes.

**Multi-state probate is also a possibility.** If you own property in more than one state, your family will very likely have to undergo probate in both states at the same time. Some of my clients have a main home and then a lake cabin in a neighboring state and/or a winter home in the south. If this describes you, in the absence of appropriate planning your family would be required to undergo probate in both states, usually simultaneously. This adds additional time, expense and aggravation.

**Conclusion.** If you do not have a written estate plan, the state has one for you. A judge will decide who manages your estate and where it goes. If your children are minors, the judge will decide who manages the money for your children and they will likely receive it outright and unprotected at age 18. As mentioned in Chapter 1, a judge will also decide who will be your children's guardian. Probate will take an estimated 2%-5% or more of your gross estate, last approximately 12-16 months, depending on your circumstances, and will be completely public.

Whether you decide to do a will or a trust for your written estate plan, I think you will agree that passing away without a written estate plan - and relying on your state's default plan for you and your family - is not in the best interest of your kids.

# CHAPTER 5

# Protecting Your Family With A Written Plan: A Will

As discussed in the last chapter, in the absence of a written plan the state will decide who manages your estate, who the beneficiaries are and when they receive your assets through the probate process. Recall also that probate is expensive (estimated at 2%-5% or more of the gross estate), time-consuming (anywhere from three months to several years depending on where you live and your estate) and is public (anyone can pull your probate file as a matter of public record and see who is getting what and when, and how to contact them).

One of the biggest misunderstandings I see about estate planning is that people think that by doing a will, they avoid probate upon their passing. That is not true. If you pass away with a written will, your family will probably still have to go through the probate process. That means it will still be expensive, time-consuming and public. However, you obtain some *major advantages* by doing a will, advantages that can protect your family, particularly your kids, and make the process easier on them.

**Advantage #1: The Ability to Name Long-Term Guardians for Your Minor Children.** Recall from Chapter 2 that unless you name long-term guardians in writing, a judge will decide who the long-term guardians are for your minor children. The judge may use criteria that you would not, and may select someone who you may not have wanted. By including a provision in your will naming long-term guardians for your minor children, you get to decide who you would want to have this important role.

**Advantage #2: The Ability to Choose Your Personal Representative.** In your will, you can nominate someone in advance to be your personal representative. This means that you decide who is in charge of your affairs, rather than leaving it up to the state to decide. By doing this, you can ensure that your affairs would be managed by someone who has the ability to do it and who would also have the best interests of your family in mind. You also ensure that your personal representative would not be someone you would not want involved.

**Advantage #3: The Ability to Name Your Beneficiaries.** In your will, you can decide who you would want to receive your assets. You can also exclude anyone from receiving your assets. In the absence of this, the court decides who gets everything based on state law.

**Advantage #4: The Ability to Decide When Your Beneficiaries Receive Their Assets.** Without a written estate plan, the court will decide when your beneficiaries receive their assets. If you have minor children, the court will most likely place the assets into what is known as a Uniform Transfers to Minors

Act account and your children will most likely receive the assets outright and unprotected at the age of 18.

In your will, you can place restrictions on how and when your children would receive their inheritance. For example, I often counsel my clients to have the money managed for their children's health, education, maintenance and support – that it be used to pay for what you would have paid for them. This can include paying for school and college, starting a business, buying a first home and even helping cover wedding expenses. I typically advise against giving them free access to their entire inheritance at the age of 18. Rather, I recommend that the remaining principal be delayed until they are old enough to manage the money themselves. Additional options for safeguarding the inheritance of minor children will be covered in greater detail in Chapter 10.

**Advantage #5: The Ability to Decide Who Manages Your Assets for Your Children.** If your children are minors, you get to decide who manages the money you leave behind for them and how that money is managed. Rather than the court deciding who would manage the finances, you get to place control of your children's inheritance in the hands of someone you trust to best manage it, with specific instructions on how you want it managed.

As noted in the previous chapter, in the absence of a written plan your estate will go through the probate process. A probate judge will decide who your personal representative is, who your beneficiaries are and when those beneficiaries receive those assets. If you have minor children, the judge will also decide who will take care of your kids and how the assets you leave for your kids will be managed. Most likely, your children will receive their inheritance outright and unprotected at the age of 18.

By preparing a will, your estate most likely will still go through the probate process. However, you get the key advantages of deciding who your personal representative will be, who your children's guardian will be, when your children will get the money you leave for them, who should manage that money and how that money will be managed. It may still be expensive, time-consuming and public, but you have accomplished a great deal more to protect and take care of your kids than if you simply left it up to the court to decide everything for you and for them.

# CHAPTER 6

# Protecting Your Family While Avoiding A Courtroom: A Trust

If you would like an estate plan that offers the advantages described in the previous chapter, with the ability to also allow your family to avoid probate, then you may want to consider using a trust as your estate planning vehicle. Many people mistakenly believe that trusts are only for the very wealthy or for taxable estates. That is simply not the case. Trusts can be a good choice for many people because they offer the advantage of allowing your family to manage your affairs without the time, expense, loss of privacy and frustration of having to go to court. In its simplest form, a trust is basically just a probate avoidance tool.

To fully understand how and why trusts work the way they do, we need to revisit wills and the probate process for a moment. A will can be thought of as a set of instructions for the probate judge. A will has no legal effect until you pass away; it is simply paper. After your passing, the will would need to be located and then presented to a probate court for validation. Only after a probate court has confirmed that the will is valid does it have any legal force and effect.

Once the will is validated by the probate court, the court will then appoint the personal representative. If you nominate someone in your will to be your personal representative, and that person survives you and is willing to serve, he/she will be appointed. If the person you nominate either does not survive you or does not want to be your personal representative, the court will appoint someone else – which is why we usually suggest naming at least one alternative in case your first choice cannot do the job for whatever reason. After being appointed, the personal representative's job is to account for all of your assets, pay all of your debts, account for everything with the court and then distribute the assets to your beneficiaries according to the instructions in your will. All of this occurs under the supervision of the probate court.

I often explain the personal representative's legal authority to manage an estate as signature authority. If something were to happen to you, there is no longer a way to sign all of the paperwork necessary to transfer ownership of your assets. Whether it's the deed to your home, titles to vehicles, bank accounts, brokerage accounts, retirement accounts or credit cards, all would need someone with the legal authority to sign the paperwork necessary to transfer ownership and/or close the accounts. The probate court gives your personal representative the legal authority to sign all of the paperwork necessary to accomplish this. Probate provides a means of replacing your signature with that of the personal representative's so that your assets can be legally managed and transferred to your beneficiaries.

Revocable "living" trusts (also called revocable inter-vivos trusts), on the other hand, are like a treasure chest. Unlike a will, which has no legal force and effect until after your passing and is validated by a judge, a trust exists the moment you sign the trust instrument. It is as if a treasure chest magically appears in the middle of your dining room table. You then open the treasure chest and put everything you own into it (with a possible few exceptions) and shut the lid. While you are alive, you and your spouse are the trustees of your trust. That means you have the keys to the treasure chest. You can open the treasure chest at any time, put anything in there that you want and take anything out that you want. In the event something were to happen to you, those you have named as your successor trustee(s) get the keys to the treasure chest. They can then put anything in or take anything out pursuant to the instructions you left in your trust document. Because you already put all of your assets into the chest prior to your passing and gave someone access to the chest, there is no need to go through the probate process to obtain signature authority to transfer ownership of your assets; you did it ahead of time.

However, for a trust to work as intended, it needs to be funded. Using the treasure chest example, you need to make sure that the assets you want to be in the trust make it in the trust. That means you either need to take the time necessary to make sure all of your assets (with a few possible exceptions) are in the name of your trust or pay someone else to do it for you. If you fail to make sure that your assets are owned by your trust, your family could potentially end up back in a probate court. In my practice, we offer to either do the funding for our clients to make sure that assets get into the trust or we give them complete written instructions for moving their assets into their revocable living trust and make ourselves available to answer any questions they may have. Funding of the trust will be discussed in greater detail in the next chapter.

Parents often have a number of specific questions about trusts, such as:

## I have heard that if I have a living trust, I will lose control of my assets. Is that true?

That is not the case in my practice. When I prepare a revocable living trust for my clients, I make sure they retain complete control of everything. If for some reason you want assistance with managing your assets, your trust can be drafted to allow for someone else – whether a broker, financial advisor, accountant, etc. – to help you and/or your successor trustee(s) manage your assets. Make sure the attorney you choose drafts your trust in a manner that allows you to have control of your own assets.

## What if I want to change the trust, can I do this?

Absolutely. A revocable living trust can be amended or terminated. You can change it as often or as little as you want. Usually, the reasons you would make changes to your trust are to change who you want to manage your assets after your passing or to change who receives your assets after your passing.

## I heard that every time you take something out of your trust or buy anything, you have to go back to an attorney to have them change the trust. Is that true?

The trusts that we prepare for our clients are written in such a way that it is very simple for clients to transfer assets in or out of the trust without the need of an attorney. We also give our clients extensive written instructions on how to do this and we never charge our clients for calling with questions. Not all attorneys have this arrangement, so if you decide to have a trust prepared, make sure you find an attorney who will do the same thing for you and your family.

## My wife and I own everything jointly. If I die first, my spouse will get everything without probate. If my spouse dies first, I get everything without probate. So why do we need a trust to avoid probate, since it looks like we will avoid it?

As mentioned in Chapter 4, if you pass first, your spouse will indeed own your joint assets without probate. If your spouse passes first, you will indeed own your joint assets without probate. The problem is when the last of you passes, there will be a probate. Owning everything jointly does not avoid probate, it just puts it off until the last of you passes. Also, if for some reason you have an asset that isn't owned by both of you, like a small business or some hunting land, probate would likely be required upon your passing to transfer the asset to your spouse and then a second probate would be required upon the passing of your spouse.

For parents with minor children, the best way to avoid probate is to prepare a valid living trust and make sure it is properly funded.

## Can't I just put my children's names on our home, bank accounts and other assets and still avoid probate without a trust?

We strongly caution our clients against doing this as a means of avoiding probate. First of all, if your children are minors, they cannot become the owner of any inherited asset until they turn 18. Any assets they would receive in this manner would automatically trigger probate and would be placed into a Uniform Transfers to Minors Act (UTMA) account.

If your children are 18 or older, you have created other problems. If you put your children's names on your home, bank accounts and other assets, you've given them a share of the asset. This is considered a gift for tax purposes. If it is over the annual gift tax exclusion amount, which is currently $14,000 per year per person as of this writing, you will trigger gift tax issues. It is also important to note that if your children are applying for financial aid for college or graduate school, these assets would count against them for qualification purposes.

You may have also given away a valuable tax advantage. In general, income tax is calculated on the income you make on an asset, less deductible expenses. Let's assume you give your children a stock when it is worth $10,000 that you bought for $2,000. They then turn around and sell it for $10,000. When they sell it, they will apply the $2,000 as a deductible expense, since your gift entitles them to count your expense against the profit. Their taxable income is $8,000. If you had given them the same stock upon your passing, they would be entitled to count the fair market value that the stock was on the day of your death, $10,000, as a deductible expense. So in this case, they would owe no income tax on it. This is known as a step-up in basis. As you can see, the benefit of receiving a step-up in basis with an inherited asset can be a significant tax advantage, to be considered as part of your overall tax planning strategy. This advantage could be lost if you added your children's names to your asset.

Also, if your children were to have a creditor's claim against them, your children's creditors could seize your assets because your children's names are on them. That means you could lose stocks, savings, and so forth to your children's creditors.

If you put your children's names on the title to your home, you have huge potential problems for you and your children. If you sell the home, you and your spouse will have the capital gains exemption for the sale of your primary residence, but your children will NOT. That means they may have to pay the capital gains tax. Also, if one of your children gets divorced, it is possible that their soon to be ex-spouse could sue for the sale of the home if there are insufficient other assets to pay them out. Yes, you read that correctly, your child's soon-to-be ex-spouse could have an ownership interest in your home even if it is only your child's name on the title with you. That is because many states give spouses a marital interest in real property even if their name is not on title to the home.

To illustrate this point, I once had a client come to me for legal help. After his wife's passing, his previous attorney advised him to put his children's names on his home, bank accounts, brokerage accounts and other assets. Unfortunately, his daughter became disabled and applied for government benefits. Because she was now on title for some of her father's assets, she did not qualify for the government benefits she would have otherwise received. To further complicate the matter, his son's broker had invested with Tom Petters, infamously known as the Bernie Madoff of Minnesota. Even though the client's son knew nothing about the investments his broker made on his behalf, his father's assets were now fair game for the government officials looking to recover assets. My client's entire life savings were at risk simply because his son's name was on them. When I explained all of this to him, he could not understand why his previous attorney had advised him to do this. I told him I couldn't understand it either.

# A Special Note about Life Insurance and Trusts

Many parents name their minor children as the pay-on-death beneficiaries of their life insurance policies. This is not advisable! Your children are not old enough to legally inherit the proceeds. In the event something were to happen to you, probate would be required to administer the proceeds of your policy. The funds would be placed into an UTMA (Uniform Transfers to Minors Act) account and the court would determine who should manage the funds for the kids and how the funds would be managed. Your children would receive them outright and unprotected at age 18. That is a disaster in my view.

Some attorneys and financial advisors suggest naming the potential guardian of your children as the beneficiary of the life insurance proceeds to try to get around probate without creating a trust. I also strongly caution against this approach as well. In the event something were to happen to you, the beneficiary of the proceeds could do whatever they wanted with the money, as they inherit it without any legal restrictions on it whatsoever. I hear the Bahamas look great in January! All joking aside, whoever you select as the guardian of your children is most likely trustworthy and would have the best interests of your children in mind; after all, you would not have chosen them if that weren't the case. That being said, things can still happen to your guardian. They could get divorced, for example. Even if you took my advice from Chapter 3 and only named your sister as your guardian, in the event she were named as the beneficiary of your life insurance and were to later get divorced, her soon-to-be ex-spouse still has a claim on all of her assets – including the life insurance proceeds she inherited from you.

### Can I just name my children as the pay-on-death beneficiary of my assets and avoid probate without a trust?

Just as in the above two examples, naming your children as the pay-on-death beneficiaries of your assets may create more problems than it avoids. If your children are minors, they cannot inherit the assets until they are 18. A probate judge would have to get involved and the assets would get placed in an UTMA account. Once your children turn 18, the assets are subject to creditor's claims and divorce.

### I keep hearing about different kinds of trusts. What are they and which will help me avoid probate?

A trust can either be created while you are alive or it can be created after your passing. A trust that is created while you are alive is known as an "inter-vivos" or living trust. A trust that gets created after your passing is known as a testamentary trust. A living trust is the type we have been discussing in this chapter. A living trust will help your family avoid probate.

A testamentary trust is usually created in your will, only comes into existence after your passing and, therefore, cannot be used to avoid probate. If you choose to do a will as your written estate plan and you have minor children, I strongly suggest that your will have provisions that create a testamentary trust to hold the assets for your children until they are old enough to receive and properly manage the assets you leave for them. I need to make clear that your estate would still have to go through the probate process, which takes an estimated 12-16 months, approximately 2%-5% of the gross estate and is public. However, at the close of the probate process your will can specify that your assets go into a trust for the benefit of your minor children.

The best way to pass on assets to minor children is with the use of either a living or a testamentary trust, because they can be used to hold, manage and protect the assets until your children are old enough to responsibly manage the assets themselves. Having said that, only a properly prepared and funded living trust will protect your family from probate.

No matter which written estate plan you choose to use, whether a will or a trust, I strongly suggest that it be designed to hold, manage and protect the assets you leave for your children until they are ready to receive them. More guidance on how you can structure your plan to protect the money you leave behind for your children will be discussed in an upcoming chapter.

# CHAPTER 7

# Which Written Estate Plan Is Best For Protecting My Family? A Will vs. A Trust

Depending on who you ask, you will likely get different answers to this question. In my opinion, their answers have a lot to do with their experience, their perspective and their business. When asked, I always tell my clients that there are pros and cons to each approach and the decision of which to choose should be based on which best accomplishes their wishes.

The short answer is that wills are usually less expensive than trusts up front. There is significantly less paperwork involved for a lawyer to draft a will than to draft a similar trust, so wills tend to be less expensive. However, because of probate expenses, wills can be more expensive in the long run. And because the family has to deal with the probate process, wills tend to be more stressful for the family.

A trust is usually more expensive up front because it requires much more work for an attorney to prepare a trust and the supporting paperwork in comparison to a will. However, because a properly drafted and funded trust avoids probate, it may be cheaper in the long run. And because your family does not have to deal with the probate process, trusts tend to be less stressful for them.

Another potential benefit of a trust-based plan over a will-based plan is estate tax minimization. If you and your spouse have an estate subject to the estate tax at either the federal or state level, you may want to consider a trust rather than a will. That is because depending on how you own your assets and the probate rules in your state, accomplishing estate tax minimization with a will may require two probate proceedings – one upon the passing of the first of you, and a second upon the passing of the surviving spouse. A properly prepared and funded trust could accomplish estate tax minimization without the need for probate at all.

A will does not require you to take the time to re-title your assets; your personal representative does that for you after your passing. A trust requires that your assets be re-titled in the name of your trust so that it works as designed to avoid probate. This may require more of your time. As you can see, each option has its pros and cons.

There are some lawyers and other professionals who will only ever suggest a will. In fact, some attorneys keep a vault full of their clients' wills in part to generate follow-up probate work. I was once approached by the managing partner of a firm. He wanted to know if I would be interested in merging my practice with theirs. In the course of the conversation, I asked him whether they were a "will-based" planning firm, a "trust-based" planning firm, or if they discussed the pros and cons of each and let their clients decide. He answered that they were a "will-based" planning firm and kept the wills to generate future probate work. I ended further discussions with them.

I am frequently invited to speak to various groups about estate planning. At one event, I had just shared the story of the vault full of wills when a woman raised her hand and asked if there really was a vault full of clients' original wills; she simply could not believe it. I told her that, yes, there was. As I finished, another woman raised her hand. She turned to the woman who had just asked that question and told her, "I just retired from my job as a legal secretary at a major law firm in another state. I won't say which one, but we had offices in several states. I worked in their trusts and estates department and one of my jobs was to file and keep track of the wills in their vault. He is absolutely telling you the truth. I saw many of our attorneys do wills and then keep the originals for the express purpose of generating probate work in the future."

Now there are also those who suggest only trusts for clients, regardless of whether or not a trust is appropriate for the client. For example, the Minnesota Attorney General's Office warns consumers about the risk of being steered unnecessarily into a trust. The Attorney General's website states that, "Living trust mills …sell boilerplate living trusts, regardless of whether a living trust is appropriate….." It goes on to state that, "[s]uch products generally consist of pre-packaged, boilerplate documents that vary greatly in quality and are not customized to the particular needs of the…purchaser."

The problem with always suggesting a will or always suggesting a trust is that it may or may not be the best fit for you and your family. The only way for you to know what is the best fit for you is to fully understand the pros and the cons of each. In my practice, I will prepare either a will or a trust for my clients. I take the time to find out what is most important to you, what you want to accomplish with your planning, and then explain the pros and cons of your options to help you choose the plan that is right for you and your family.

I once met with a woman who had attended one of my presentations. She explained that several months prior, she researched estate planning options and then met with an attorney to get her estate planning done. Based on her research, she thought a trust would be best for her because it would avoid probate and make things easier for her adult children. However, the attorney she met with dismissed her inclination to go with a trust and insisted that she go with a will-based plan instead.

She went on to explain that after she attended my presentation, she did additional research and again felt that a trust would be the best fit for her and her family. She then scheduled a follow-up meeting with the attorney who prepared her will. The attorney again insisted on a will for her. At that point, she asked him, "Are you an estate planning attorney or a probate lawyer?" She said he sat back in his chair and said nothing. At that point she decided it wasn't a good fit and scheduled an appointment with our office.

During our meeting, she shared with me what had happened. I still took the next hour to walk through the pros and cons of a will and a trust, and how each might work for her and her family. When we were done, she thanked me for taking the time to explain all of her options. She said that my explanation confirmed her research and she had decided to have me prepare a trust for her because she felt that ultimately it was the best choice for her and her family.

If you meet with an attorney who will not take the time to explain all of your options to you, and explain the pros and cons of each, then find a different attorney who will. What may be the right plan for someone else may be entirely wrong for you and your family. The only way to know what is the best approach for you and your family is to thoroughly discuss all the options, guided by what is most important to you.

# CHAPTER 8

# Making Sure You Leave Enough For Your Kids

In the event something were to happen to you, it is important to leave enough money to take care of your children, either through savings or through life insurance. Each year, the U.S. Department of Agriculture releases a report stating what the average middle-income family would spend to raise a child born that year to the age of 18. According to the report released in August of 2013, that number was $241,080 ($301,970 with projected inflation). It should be noted that this figure does not include the cost of college. The report also noted that for families making more than $100,000 in combined household income, the cost was $399,780.

If you do not have sufficient money saved to provide for your children in the event something were to happen to you – and based on these numbers many of us don't – then you need to consider life insurance. There are many different types of life insurance available to you. To determine what type of life insurance and what amounts are appropriate for you and your family, I strongly suggest meeting with a qualified financial advisor.

That being said, here is a process I go through with my clients to help them determine how much life insurance they may need:

**Online Calculators May Be Inadequate.** The first thing to note is that online calculators based on income are often inadequate shortcuts. For example, a family of four with a stay-at-home mom, two young children and a mortgage may need significantly more life insurance than a couple with two working spouses, two teenage children and no mortgage - even if household income is the same for both families.

**Plan to cover the expenses of a funeral.** On average, funeral and burial expenses are estimated at $6,000-$7,000. However, they can run $10,000 or more. Include this in your estimate.

**Your mortgage and any other debts.** Figure out the total of your mortgage, student loans, car loans and any other significant debts you have. Your family may decide not to pay off these items and some of your debts may be forgiven with your passing. The last thing you want, though, is for your family to be forced to sell your home or other cherished asset because they had no choice as a result of your passing.

**Education expenses for your children.** Would you like to cover all of your children's college educations or just a portion? Once you decide that, take a look at the current costs of some of the schools you and/or your children may be considering. College costs have been rising steadily each year. Based on this and the ages of your children, you should be able to determine how much you want to set aside for them.

**Income replacement.** If something were to happen to you, your family would need to replace your lost income. To do this, figure out what your current pre-tax income is and then determine how many years of lost income you would like to replace for your family in the event something were to happen to you. Is it just until your children would graduate from high school or until they graduate from college? Or, would you like to replace your income from your current age until your planned retirement age? Or some other age entirely?

Also, don't forget to replace the income of a stay-at-home parent. I often get a good laugh from my clients when I mention this to them. They usually tell me "anything times zero is still zero." Mathematically, they are correct. However, consider the following: If a stay-at-home parent were to pass away unexpectedly, you may now have to pay for daycare and/or a nanny. The stay-at-home parent probably also does most, if not all, of the grocery and other shopping, takes the kids to and from school, swimming lessons, dance class, sports and the host of other after-school and extracurricular activities, probably assists with a greater amount of the children's homework and may do a majority of the housework. Now, pause for a moment and ask yourself how much it would cost for you to either take time away from your current job to do this (if you even could) or to hire someone to do all of that. Make sure you factor that into your model as well.

These numbers are all amounts to consider when determining how much life insurance to get. You may also need to tweak these numbers based on your personal circumstances. For example, if your spouse or one of your children has a medical condition, you may need more. If you have a special needs child, you may need more. If you and/or your spouse have a good salary and some savings, you may need less. By going through this exercise, you will have a pretty good idea how much life insurance you would need to take care of your children in the event something were to happen to you.

For most families, the amount of life insurance they discover they need is usually large and may even be a little frightening. It doesn't have to be. I usually suggest that clients obtain, at a minimum, a term life insurance policy in the amount(s) they need, and for the period they need, based on this exercise. Term insurance can be very inexpensive; a $1 million 20-year term policy can often be purchased for less than a thousand dollars a year.

This exercise should help give you an idea of how much you would need to take care of your children in the event anything were to happen to you. That being said, I highly suggest you take the time to discuss your specific needs with a qualified financial planner who can help you decide exactly how much and what type of insurance you need to protect your family in the way that you would want.

# CHAPTER 9

# Providing For Your Children Instead Of The Government: Estate Taxes

Benjamin Franklin famously quipped, "The only two certainties in life are death and taxes." I guess he never imagined the modern tax code where they managed to effectively combine the two.

## The Politics Behind the Federal Estate Tax

There is no way to discuss estate taxes (also known as death taxes) without also discussing politics. In general terms, and this is painting with a broad brush, Republicans do not like estate taxes and Democrats do. At the federal level, this has resulted in a political compromise that I affectionately call the "great mess."

There is a number out there and, if the total value of your estate at the time of your death is below this number, your estate is not subject to federal estate taxes. If the total value of your estate is above this number at the time of your passing, your estate will be subject to estate taxes.

Planning is difficult, though, because the number keeps changing. In 1997, that number was $600,000. It was $1 million in 2002, $2 million in 2006 and then $3.5 million in 2009. In 2010, it disappeared entirely as part of a political compromise. That's right, in the year 2010 there was no federal estate tax. George Steinbrenner, the former billionaire owner of the New York Yankees, passed away in 2010. His family saved a bundle on federal estate taxes.

As part of the political compromise, in 2011 the federal estate tax resurfaced with a $1 million exemption. However, Congress and President Obama decided to raise the exemption to $5 million – but for only two years. On January 1, 2013, the federal estate tax exemption was again lowered to $1 million as a result of a sunset provision. However, as part of the so-called "fiscal cliff" negotiations, the President and Congress agreed to raise the exemption to $5.25 million with future indexing for inflation. However, with the stroke of a pen, they could change it again. As you can see, it is exceedingly hard to plan when you don't know whether or not your estate will be taxable at your death.

## The Problems with Portability

The federal estate tax also includes a portability provision. Portability allows a surviving spouse to use any unused exemption from their deceased spouse's estate without the need for any additional planning. In layman's terms, that means a married couple can double the amount of their estate that escapes federal estate tax without the need to do any planning in advance. It is like a get-out-jail-free card for federal estate taxes.

It is important, though, to keep in mind that portability has a number of shortcomings and relying on it may lead to traps for those who fail to plan. For example, with the stroke of a pen portability could disappear and if a spouse pre-deceased, you could find you have now lost the ability to maximize the amount of money that you could pass free of estate taxes. Because portability is a federal law, it may not apply to estate taxes in your state of residence. That means if your estate is subject to estate taxes in your state of residence, portability may not protect you. For example, as of this writing, portability does not apply to state-level estate taxes in my home state of Minnesota. Portability also does not protect your surviving spouse in the event they remarry, have a creditor's claim or need medical assistance. Finally, portability does not protect the money you leave for your children from their creditors and failed marriages.

A trust-based estate plan offers the benefit of portability, but with many other advantages as well. It can protect the assets of a surviving spouse and heirs in the event a spouse remarries, since in many states a new spouse has an immediate claim to a portion of the estate unless steps were taken ahead of time to protect it. A trust-based estate plan also protects your children's inheritance from creditors, predators and failed marriages. Unless you take the time to set up a proper trust to hold and manage the money for your children, their creditors and spouse may have claims on their inheritance.

A properly prepared trust can also work to protect assets from your spouse's creditors and/or Medicaid spend-down requirements.

A trust can help protect your estate from state estate taxes in the event you reside in a state with a separate state estate tax, since portability may not apply to the estate tax in your state.

# State Estate Taxes

Many states, such as my home state of Minnesota, also have their own estate taxes with varying exemptions. That makes it even more difficult to plan, because you don't know for certain whether or not your estate will be taxable at all, taxable only at the state level, taxable only at the federal level or potentially taxable at both levels due to the ongoing politics surrounding the estate tax.

# Planning Around Estate Taxes

If the total value of your estate upon your passing will definitely be under both the federal and state estate tax exemptions, you may not need to do any estate tax planning. However, if the total value of your estate will be over either the federal or state estate tax exemptions, you need to do some planning if you want to pass the maximum amount tax free to your children.

With that background, we need to make an assumption or two just to show you how you can plan around estate taxes to take care of your kids instead of taking care of the government. The first assumption we are going to make is that you are subject to state estate taxes and that the state estate taxes apply to estates over $1 million in total estate value. The second assumption is that the state estate taxes you are subject to do not have portability. We are choosing $1 million for illustration purposes only. The actual exemption amount above which your estate may be subject to estate taxes is of course dependent on state laws applicable to you as well as the exemption amount that Congress and the President settle on at any given point in time for federal estate taxes.

When I am speaking to a group or meeting with clients, often someone will say to me, "but we don't have anywhere near a $1 million estate." Then one of two things occurs: 1) they discover they do have a $1 million estate after adding up the value of everything they own; and/or 2) they have a million dollar estate after they've done the exercise from the last chapter and purchased an appropriate amount of life insurance. The follow up is usually, "but my agent told me life insurance proceeds are not taxable." That is only partially true. Life insurance proceeds may be exempt from income taxes. However, if the policy is owned by your estate at the time of your passing, they are includable in your gross estate to determine whether or not you have a taxable estate for estate tax purposes.

Because my home state of Minnesota has a separate state estate tax with an exemption amount that, as of this writing, is significantly lower than the federal exemption, our clients often find that once they have an appropriate level of life insurance to take care of their children in the event something were to happen to them, they will have a taxable estate. If you reside in a state that has a separate estate tax, you may find that your estate is taxable at the state level even if it would not be taxable at the federal level.

Let us now also assume for illustration purposes that you and your spouse live in a state that only has a $1 million estate tax exemption, and that when you add up the value of everything you own – your home, your retirement accounts, your savings accounts, and your life insurance – that you and your spouse have a combined estate of $2 million upon your passing. Under current law, you can pass an unlimited amount to your surviving spouse, estate tax free. So upon the passing of the first spouse, the entire estate can pass to the surviving spouse estate tax free; there is no tax at the first death. However, now the surviving spouse has an estate that is valued at $2 million. When the surviving spouse passes away, the first million would not be subject to the state's estate tax and would pass to the children free of estate taxes. However, the second million would be subject to the state's estate tax.

There are ways around this, though. Under current law, you and your spouse each have a separate exemption, but you have to use it or you can lose it. Remember, as of this writing, federal portability does not apply to state estate taxes in Minnesota and may not apply in your state.

If you have taken the time to do the proper planning in advance, upon the passing of the first spouse you can put a portion of the estate into a treasure chest – a trust – of which you, as the surviving spouse, are the trustee; you have the key to the box. The surviving spouse and children can have access to the income and principal of that trust based on certain standards allowed under the law. So long as those standards are maintained, the law treats it as the assets of your deceased spouse and not yours.

In this way, you double the exemption amount in existence at the time of the passing of your spouse. In our example, that means $2 million is protected from state estate taxes instead of just $1 million. If the estate tax rate in your state is 10%, that means you have passed an additional $100,000 to your children that would otherwise have been lost to estate taxes. If you have a larger estate, or a higher tax rate in your state, the savings could be even larger. As you can see, it pays to plan.

It is important to understand that you can do this planning with either a will and testamentary trust as your written estate plan or with a revocable living trust. Will-based planning may require probate before the testamentary trust comes into existence to hold the assets, whereas a revocable living trust will avoid probate.

Either way, you have doubled the amount of your estate that escapes estate taxes by utilizing a properly drafted and funded trust that was either created prior to your passing or that comes into existence via your will after your passing.

## Planning Beyond the Exemption Amount

If your estate, even with the additional exemption from this type of planning, would still be taxable at either the state or the federal level, or even possibly both, you can still work around the estate tax. It just requires some additional planning.

Up until this point, whenever we discussed a trust we were discussing a revocable trust; a trust that you can change at any time you want, that you can put anything into or take anything out of at any time.

Additional planning to avoid estate taxes often requires the use of an irrevocable trust. Unlike a living trust, once an irrevocable trust is set up you can only change it under very limited circumstances. Because the trust cannot be changed once it is set up, along with some other technical details that are beyond the scope of this book, assets that get placed into an irrevocable trust can be effectively removed from your estate entirely for the purposes of estate taxes.

That means that assets you place into an irrevocable trust are removed from your estate and may avoid estate taxes. As a result, it is possible to take assets over and above the estate tax exemption amount, put them into an irrevocable trust for the benefit of a surviving spouse and/or children, and have those assets avoid estate taxes.

One such irrevocable trust that you may find useful for providing for your children is an irrevocable life insurance trust. If, after taking advantage of the planning that allows you to double your exemption amount you still have a taxable estate as a result of your life insurance, you can consider placing your policies into an irrevocable life insurance trust ("ILIT"). A properly prepared ILIT will allow you to remove the proceeds of your life insurance policy from your estate for estate tax purposes, while still allowing the proceeds to be made available for your surviving spouse and children. A properly prepared ILIT may also be used to provide money to your family to pay estate taxes for those estates that would still be taxable after doubling your exemption.

Irrevocable trusts are an advanced estate planning tool and you should seek competent financial and legal advice before using one. Planning around estate taxes also requires competent financial and legal advice to help guide you and your family through the available options. That being said, the benefits of including estate tax minimization in your plan often make these advanced estate planning strategies a wise investment.

If you want to provide for your children, you need to consider the effects of the estate tax on your estate. If you fail to take into account estate taxes, you may leave your children hundreds of thousands of dollars short of the money they may need. By planning ahead, you can help ensure that your children receive more of your hard-earned money if anything ever happened to you.

# CHAPTER 10

# Protecting Your Children's Inheritance

A colleague of mine shared the following story with me over lunch one day. While he was in law school, he had a job as a clerk in the Probate Court for the largest county in Minnesota. One morning, just after the office opened, a young man approached the counter. My friend asked how he could help him. The young man proceeded to explain that today was his 18th birthday and that he was here to pick up the remaining money that the court was managing for him since the passing of his parents. My friend took his identification, determined the details, and after the appropriate paperwork, handed the young man a check for the balance of his account. When he did so, he asked the young man what he planned to do with the money: go to college, start a business, etc. The young man told him he was heading straight over to one of the "gentlemen's clubs" a few blocks away. I wonder how long it took him to spend all of it?

Many of us probably know or have read a similar story of someone inheriting a sum of money and then promptly losing all of it. With careful planning, this does not have to happen to your children.

The first step in that planning is to set up either a testamentary or revocable living trust to hold and manage the money you leave for your kids. Remember, unless you take the time to provide how and when the money you leave behind will be received by your children, a probate judge will decide, and your children will likely receive their inheritance outright and unprotected at the age of 18.

The next step in that process is to select someone, or a couple of people, to manage that money for your children. You want to select someone who is a responsible money manager. You may even consider requiring that the person you name to manage the money for your kids hire a certified financial planner or other professional money manager to assist them in the investment and management of the money under their care.

Next, make sure to provide clear instructions on how the money is to be managed. Those instructions usually include provisions to provide for your children's health, education, maintenance and welfare – provide money that you would have provided. Depending on your wishes, provisions can also be included that would allow the funds to be used to help pay for a child's wedding, start a business, travel abroad or to purchase a first home.

You may also want to ensure that the children do not receive the remaining principal outright at age 18. Rather, we suggest you pick an age or a couple of ages, or significant markers, when they can receive some or all of the remaining principal. For example, some clients choose to release a portion of the principal at one age and then the remaining principal at a later age; say, half at age

25 and the remaining balance at age 30. Sometimes the ages are 25, 30, 35. Sometimes the ages are 30 and 40.

Other clients will select events in their children's lives, such as receiving their bachelor's degree. For example, some of my clients release the first half upon the earlier of their child receiving their bachelor's degree or age 25. In one case, I had a client specify that her son's inheritance was to go into an annuity that he could not access until his 62nd birthday, except in extreme circumstances. She said her son was a spendthrift and that if she didn't do it that way, he would never have a retirement. It is up to you what you choose. The important point is that your children not receive their money until they are old enough to manage it wisely.

Finally, consider adding asset protection provisions. What if, when they reach a marker for receiving their inheritance, one of your children has an event going on in their lives that could cause them to lose it? For example, what if your plan specifies that your child not receive the balance of their inheritance until they reach the age of 30 but upon reaching that age, they have a creditor's claim against them or a substance abuse issue or are getting a divorce? You didn't set aside money to take care of your children only to have it lost to a creditor, your child's substance abuse issue or their soon-to-be ex-spouse.

That is why I suggest your plan include provisions that state that in the event your child has any of these events going on in their lives, or any other event that the person you named to manage the money for your child believes would cause them to immediately lose the funds if given to them, the funds remain in trust until that issue has resolved itself. I call this protecting your children's inheritance from creditors and failed marriages. If you have minor children, you should consider having these protections built into your plan. You may also want to consider a beneficiary-controlled dynasty trust. A beneficiary-controlled dynasty trust can take these provisions even a step further by protecting your children's inheritance from creditors, predators and failed marriages throughout their lifetime rather than just at specific ages or mile markers.

# CHAPTER 11

# In Case You Are Ever Incapacitated: Financial Powers Of Attorney

Do you know who would manage your financial affairs in the event of your incapacity? If something were to happen to you and/or your spouse, a court may need to appoint a guardian or conservator to help manage your financial affairs. Rather than leave the decisions up to a judge and incur the time and expense of a court proceeding, you should have a financial power of attorney that appoints someone of your choosing to help manage your financial affairs in the event of your incapacity.

In most states, a spouse is automatically in charge in the event of your incapacity. However, what if your spouse is also incapacitated? Who has the authority to deal with your insurance company, pay the mortgage and make your other payments? Perhaps you are thinking you took care of this by preparing a will or trust?

The first thing you need to know about financial powers of attorney is that they are not a replacement for a valid will or trust. The second thing you need to understand about financial powers of attorney is that your will or trust is not a replacement for them either. A financial power of attorney supplements your will or trust, but does not replace it. Remember, a will has no legal effect until you pass away. Until you pass away, it is just paper. A trust takes effect immediately and your trust can provide for a successor trustee to step in and manage trust assets during your incapacity. However, the trustee could only manage the assets inside of the trust. In the event that any of your financial matters were not inside of your trust, the successor trustee would have no legal control over them.

That is why everyone should have a written financial power of attorney specifying who has the legal authority to manage your financial matters in the event of your incapacity. The person you name as having this authority is known as your agent. The financial power of attorney should also list the powers your agent has as well as any restrictions you want to place on those powers.

In the absence of a written financial power of attorney, your family could end up in court to gain the necessary authority to manage your financial affairs.

# CHAPTER 12

# Making Difficult Decisions Easier For Your Family:Health Care Directives (Living Wills)

If you watched the news or read a newspaper at any point between 1998 and 2005, you probably heard of Terri Schiavo. In February of 1990 Terri Schiavo collapsed in her Florida home and fell into a coma. As a result of oxygen deprivation, she suffered severe brain damage and was later diagnosed as being in a persistent vegetative state. In 1998, her husband petitioned a Florida court to remove her feeding tube. Terri's parents sought to block the removal.

Numerous state and federal court hearings followed as well as the passage of federal legislation that President George W. Bush flew back into Washington just to sign. When it was all said and done, Terri Schiavo's case involved 14 different appeals and hearings in Florida courts, five suits in federal court, Florida legislation that was struck down by the Florida Supreme Court, federal legislation and four denials for hearing before the United States Supreme Court. Terri Schiavo passed away on March 31, 2005. All of it could have been avoided if Terri Schiavo had a health care directive, also known as a living will.

A health care directive serves two purposes. The first is to name who you want to make health care decisions for you in the event you are unable to express your wishes. This person is known as your health care agent. The second is to list your instructions for your health care agent so that they know what you want for your care.

In most states, a spouse is automatically your health care agent even if you do not have a written health care directive. That being said, if for any reason you would not want your spouse to be your health care agent, then you would want to have a written health care directive wherein you make clear who you would want instead. Even if you would want your spouse to be your health care agent, you should still have a written living will naming at least one alternative in case your spouse is unable to act as your agent for any reason.

You also want to provide clear written instructions about your health care wishes for your agent. In the absence of instructions, your health care agent and/or your family may not know what to do if difficult decisions for your care need to be made. Terri Schiavo's case illustrates what can happen when your spouse believes you wanted one course of action for your treatment and your family believes you would have wanted something else. In court proceedings, Terri Schiavo's husband said that he and Terry had discussed her wishes and she told him that she would never want to be kept alive by machines. Terri's parents stated that Terri was a devout Catholic and would not want any form of euthanasia; she would want to fight for every chance to be alive. Who was right? It's difficult to know for certain because Terri never put her wishes for her care in writing.

Also, when you leave your instructions, make sure they are as thorough as possible and cover the various scenarios your health care agent may have to face. For example, if you were in a terminal condition, would you want treatment to continue or would you want to be made as comfortable as possible and allowed to pass? What care would you want if you were diagnosed as in a persistent vegetative state? What would you want to have happen if you were pregnant but diagnosed as terminal or had been in an accident and would never recover but your unborn baby could survive? What care and treatment would you want if you had some sort of worsening mental and physical condition that perhaps was not terminal, but then you were to have an accident of some sort; for example, you had a heart attack while suffering from Alzheimer's and/or dementia? Would you want to be resuscitated under those circumstances? If you did want care and treatment, what types and for how long? Would you want mechanical respiration? Tube feeding? The clearer and more complete your instructions, the easier it will be on the person you ask to make these decisions and the easier it will be on your family – they will know that the decision being made by your agent is indeed what you wanted.

The importance of your written instructions to your family cannot be understated. I had a couple come to me to assist with their estate planning. The wife had been diagnosed with terminal cancer and wanted everything taken care of in advance to make things as easy as possible for her family. In her health care directive, she specified that she wanted her husband as her agent and took the time to write down her wishes for her care. When she was comatose and close to death, the hospital informed the family that they had done all they could do and suggested hospice. Pursuant to her wishes, her husband took her home so that she could pass away in her own bed surrounded by her family. Her parents could not believe that was what she wanted. When her husband showed them her written instructions, it helped relieve his own stress in knowing that he was following her wishes and helped to minimize stress and tension with his in-laws. Saying goodbye is never easy. The easier you can make it on your family, the better.

You also need to understand HIPAA and how it applies to you and your family. Recall from the discussion in Chapter 3 that the Health Insurance Portability and Accountability Act – HIPAA – protects your medical information from third parties. The law was initially passed in 1996 and later provisions were added for the protection of medical information; these provisions went into full effect in April of 2003. I am seeing many health care directives that are not HIPAA compliant, meaning that the health care directive does not expressly give the health care agent authority under HIPAA to gain access to needed medical information. If your health care directive is not HIPAA compliant, it means the person you name as your health care agent may not be able to get access to your medical records or receive information from medical personnel that they would need to make decisions for your health care.

In one case in California, a woman was named as her mother's health care agent in her health care directive. However, the directive did not have the necessary HIPAA authorization in it. When her mother was hospitalized, her daughter had to go to court to get access to information about her mother's medical condition in order to make decisions for her.

A health care directive helps both you and your family. The clearer and more complete your instructions are for your agent, the easier it will be on them and your family.

# CHAPTER 13

# What Do You Mean Doctors Can't Automatically Consult With Me During An Emergency Once My Kids Turn 18?! (Planning for College Students)

The majority of this book has been dedicated to protecting your minor children in the event something were to happen to you. But what happens when your children become adults?

You may be paying your children's college tuition and expenses and may even have them on your health insurance. But, once your children turn 18, they are now legally adults. And just because you are their parent and even if you are still responsible for helping pay for your children, your legal rights as their parent and your legal relationship with your children have forever changed.

Your college-bound children should have three important documents:

**A health care directive/living will.** This document should authorize you to make decisions regarding your child's medical care in the event they are unable to make decisions themselves. In addition, this should include HIPAA authority for you so that you have access to medical information you would need to help your child during an emergency.

I recently read about a mom who learned about HIPAA the hard way. She had received a call from a friend of her daughter's letting her know that her daughter had been involved in a car accident five hours away at college. When she called the hospital to check on her daughter, she learned that due to HIPAA, the hospital could not share any information with her about her daughter unless she had a signed authorization granting her HIPAA agent rights.

Not long ago, our oldest daughter had oral surgery to assist with her orthodontic treatment. As we sat in the waiting room for her procedure to be completed, a young woman was called by the nurse to come to the back. As the young woman and her mother approached the door, the nurse held out her hand and blocked the mom from coming in. She then explained that since the young woman was 18, her mom could only come back if the young woman wanted her to. The young woman said yes and her mom followed her back. Some minutes later the mom returned to the waiting room while her daughter was having her procedure. I couldn't help but think that in the event there were any complications during the surgery, this mom was not authorized to gain any information about her daughter, nor authorized to make any medical decisions for her.

**A financial power of attorney.** A financial power of attorney will allow you to manage your child's financial affairs in the event they are unable to do so themselves. This would authorize you to, among other things, help pay bills and to open and close accounts as necessary. It would also authorize you to deal with your son or daughter's college when getting questions answered about things like tuition and, yes, in many cases, even grades.

**A will.** With a child at age 18, you are still probably highly involved with helping prepare your child for the future. Getting a will in place for them now will allow them to have this important document in hand for years to come, with the occasional modification for life events and other updates.

Once your children turn 18 and head off to college, it is a good idea to send them off with a health care directive, a financial power of attorney and a will of their own. That way, it is clear that you have power of attorney to manage their financial affairs and to make health care decisions for your child. And a side benefit is that a properly drafted power of attorney may allow you access to your child's college grades – never a bad thing.

# CHAPTER 14

# Planning For Your Special Needs Child

If you are the parent of a special needs child, then you need particular planning to care for your child. As you already know, special needs children require greater care than those without special needs. That means you need to plan to leave additional resources to take care of your child in the event of your passing. In addition, you need to ensure that the resources you leave are not only protected, but that they also do not cause your child to lose the government benefits they will need.

In the absence of proper planning, anything your child inherits could cause them to lose their government benefits. For example, if your child were receiving government benefits due to their disability and were to inherit from your estate, the inheritance could cause them to lose the disability assistance. Your child might then need to spend the inherited assets and then reapply for government assistance.

Your child will require a supplemental needs trust. A supplemental needs trust is a special trust that holds assets to supplement, rather than replace, the resources your child does or will receive from governmental sources. Rather than allowing your special needs child to inherit outright, you design your estate plan so that any assets your child would receive are directed into a supplemental needs trust for their benefit.

You would then name a trustee to manage those assets along with providing specific instructions for how the assets are to be managed. The trustee can then use those assets to supplement benefits your child receives from the government. The rules on the use and management of supplemental needs trust assets are very specific. For example, the trustee cannot give any money directly to your child. Instead, the trustee must provide the assets directly to the store or service provider.

There are a couple of ways to fund a supplemental needs trust. Some parents choose to split their estate equally among all of their children, with the portion of the estate that would otherwise go to their special needs child going instead into their supplemental needs trust. Some parents will choose to leave a larger portion, sometimes even all of their estate, to benefit their special needs child. Other parents will provide for their special needs child by purchasing a life insurance policy on either or both their lives, with the proceeds directed into the supplemental needs trust for their child. The remaining assets would be split among the rest of their children. Whatever method you choose to fund the trust, you just need to make sure there are sufficient assets in there to supplement your child's care, and to make sure the trust is specifically drafted so as to not cause your child to lose their government benefits.

Even if you do not have a special needs child now, you may want to consider having provisions in your estate plan that provide for the creation of a supplemental needs trust in the event your children later develop a disability. This way, if any of your children become disabled later, the money you leave for them would not cause them to lose government benefits that they may need and would otherwise qualify for.

Finally, if you are the parent of a special needs child, your parents' estate plan could cause problems for your son or daughter. If your parents' plan potentially leaves anything to your son or daughter, and MOST DO, it could cause your child to lose any benefits they receive now or in the future. You and/or your attorney will need to talk to your parents to make sure their estate plan is drafted to direct anything that might otherwise go to your special needs child into your child's supplemental needs trust. And, in the event your parents do not have a written estate plan, most state laws provide a number of ways in which your children could inherit from them, particularly if you happened to pass away before either or both of your parents. In the event your parents do not have a written estate plan, or even if they do, you need to make sure their plan, or lack of a plan, does not cause your child to lose their government benefits.

As a closing note, planning for children with special needs is a very particular area of the law. If you are the parent of a special needs child, you need to take the time to find an attorney who has experience in this area to prepare your estate plan.

# CHAPTER 15

# Special Considerations For Blended Families

If you and/or your spouse have children from a prior relationship, then your estate planning is more complicated than you may realize. You might be surprised to learn where state law directs your assets to go if you do not have a written estate plan in place. Also, complications can arise because blended families tend to litigate estates far more often than more traditional families, resulting in dissent and discord. Therefore, it is even more important that you take the time to get a plan in place to help protect your children from future disagreements. It will be far easier on your children if you plan ahead of time, rather than forcing them and the probate court to decide for you after the fact.

The first thing you need to understand is that you and your spouse can each have your own separate estate plan. It doesn't matter if you have been married for a very short time or for a very long time. It doesn't matter if you own everything jointly or if you own significant assets in your individual name; each of you can have your own estate plan. That means each of you can separately decide who manages your affairs and who is given the authority to make health care decisions on your behalf in an emergency, among other things.

Remember, each state has default rules about what happens to your assets in the event you pass away without a written estate plan. Recall also that most people are surprised to find out what those rules are and what happens to their assets. This is especially true for blended families. I will give you an example of what currently happens in my home state of Minnesota to illustrate this – though your state and its rules may be different.

Imagine for a moment that you have children from a prior relationship, own a home and remarry. Imagine also that your new spouse also has children from a prior relationship. After the marriage, your new spouse moves into your home with you. If you were to pass away without a will, Minnesota law specifies that your spouse would be entitled to continue living in your home for the rest of their life. They would also be entitled to a family allowance of up to $1,500 per month for either one year or eighteen months out of your assets. Your spouse would also be entitled to household and personal effects up to $10,000 and one automobile. In addition to everything listed, your spouse would be entitled to the first $150,000 of the "intestate estate" and one half of the balance of the "intestate estate." The intestate estate is defined in Minnesota law as the total property you owned at your passing, excluding the items your spouse already received. In summary, here is everything your new spouse would be entitled to if you passed away without a will:

1. The right to live in your home for the rest of their life. Only after your new spouse passes could the home be sold and your kids receive any proceeds. If your spouse moved out

and the home were sold prior to their passing, your spouse would have a right to a portion of the sales proceeds.

2. Personal effects up to $10,000 and one automobile.

3. An allowance of up to $1,500 per month for up to 18 months.

4. The first $150,000 of the remainder of your estate.

5. One half of the balance of your estate.

You should also be aware that if your estate required probate, your new spouse would have preference for being named as the personal representative/executor of your estate under state law. Also, if you became incapacitated and needed someone to make financial and health care decisions for you, your spouse would have the legal right to make all of those decisions without having to consult with your kids.

Now, this might be exactly what you would want. But there may be situations where you might not want this arrangement. Maybe you have a close relationship with your kids and feel they would be more knowledgeable about your health care wishes than your new spouse. Maybe your new spouse is financially established and you would rather direct more money to your kids. Without a written estate plan, your wishes might not be honored.

If you passed away with a written will, some things change but not as much as you might think. Your new spouse would still have the right to live in your home for the rest of their life, even if your will left it to your kids. Your new spouse would also be entitled to a family allowance of up to $1,500 per month for either one year or 18 months. Your spouse would still be entitled to household and personal effects up to $10,000 and one automobile. The difference is in what happens to the balance.

Rather than automatically receiving the first $150,000 and one half of the balance, your new spouse would receive whatever else you left for him/her in your will, with one caveat: If your spouse does not believe that you provided them with enough of the balance, if they did not feel they received their "fair share" after everything else, they would have the legal right to seek an "elective share" of the balance of your estate. How much of the balance they could receive would depend upon how long the two of you had been married. The elective share varies from 3% to 50% of the balance of the estate based on the number of years you were married. In summary, here is everything your new spouse would be entitled to if you passed away with a will, based on Minnesota law:

1.  The right to live in your home for the rest of their life. Only after your spouse passed could the home be sold and your kids receive their share of any proceeds. If your spouse moved out and the home were sold prior to his/her passing, they would have a right to a portion of the sales proceeds.

2.  Personal effects up to $10,000 and one automobile.

3.  An allowance of up to $1,500 per month for up to 18 months.

4.  Whatever else you left your spouse in your will. However, if they feel they did not receive their "fair share" of the balance, they can seek an elective share between 3% to 50% of the balance of your estate based on the number of years you were married.

As you can see, based on the nature of your assets and the total value of your estate when you passed, the majority of it could end up going to your spouse. Again, this may be exactly the way you want it. One important thing to note, though, is that when your spouse passes away, they would be free to pass the value of what they inherited from you to their own kids and to the exclusion of yours. Yes, you read that right – everything your spouse inherits from you could be given to your spouse's own children and yours would have no legal right to it. That means special family heirlooms or even a piece of land such as a family farm or cabin that had been in the family for generations could end up going to the new spouse's family instead of your own. However, by planning in advance, you could protect your assets and make sure that more of them – even all of them – would go to your children at your passing.

If you would not want the default rules to apply to your blended family, then you need to put a plan in place that ensures that your wishes would be followed in the event anything ever happened to you. Here are some of the questions you and your spouse also need to ask yourselves. Your answers to these questions will go a long way in deciding what your estate plans look like.

**Should each of you treat all of the children equally in your planning, or should you give them different amounts?** If you have children from a prior relationship and children with your new spouse, you will need to decide which children receive what and from whom. You and your spouse could choose to treat all of your children as your joint children in your estate plans. Or, you could decide to provide a certain amount for your children from your prior relationship, with your current spouse providing nothing for those children in their estate plan, and then each of you provide for your joint children in your plans. You could provide different amounts to children who are adults than children who are minors. However you arrange this is up to you, as long as you document your decision in writing in your estate plan. Failing to do so could mean that your family ends up in a long, expensive argument that eventually gets decided by a judge.

**What if you paid for college for older children, but have not yet paid for younger ones – how should you account for this?** Again, each of you can decide as part of your individual estate plan how you want to provide for your children. There is no right or wrong answer. However, you do need to decide how each of you will address the issue in your planning. Many of my clients choose to include an additional amount to the younger children to help with college expenses.

**Should you leave everything for your surviving spouse or should you protect a portion of your estate for your children from your prior relationship?** Again, there is no right or wrong answer. You could decide to leave your entire estate to your surviving spouse, which may mean your children from your prior relationship would receive nothing. Or, you could decide to leave a portion of your estate to your children from your prior relationship and a portion to your surviving spouse. If you and your spouse have children together, you could leave money for your surviving spouse, your joint children, your children from your prior relationship and/or your spouse's children from a prior relationship. The important thing is that whatever you want to happen, that you get it included in a written estate plan rather than let a court decide and create dissent and discord in your family.

The following are examples of blended families that I have worked with over the years. Their names and some of the details have been changed to protect their identities. How these families handled their plans can hopefully provide some guidance to you and your spouse as you do your own.

**Greg and Rhonda.** Greg and Rhonda have three small children together. Rhonda also has a son from a previous relationship. Rhonda's son is several years older than her three small children.

<u>What they did</u>. Rhonda's estate plan provides that upon her passing, a small portion of her estate goes into a separate trust for her son to help cover his living and college expenses. The remainder of her estate is left to her husband to manage as he sees fit for himself and their three children. Should her husband pre-decease her, the portion that would have otherwise gone to her husband is held in trust for her other three children with distributions at ages 25 and 30 with asset protection.

The amount Rhonda put into trust for her son is not large because she knows that her son's father will also be providing for him. Greg is named as the trustee of that account because she does not want her son's father to end up controlling the money. Rhonda specified that the proceeds be managed for her son's health, education, maintenance and welfare. Any principal remaining is to be distributed one-half at age 25 and the remaining balance at age 30 with asset protection provisions on her son's inheritance. Should her son pass away before the trust balance is used, the remainder would go to her and Greg's joint children. Greg's plan leaves nothing to Rhonda's son and has everything being managed for the benefit of their three joint children.

**Grant and Margaret.** Grant and Margaret each have two children from a previous relationship. They do not have any children together.

<u>What they did</u>. Grant and Margaret have each set up their estate plans so that upon the passing of one of them, their home and part of the estate of the spouse who passed is left for the benefit

of the surviving spouse. The remaining portion of the estate of the spouse who passed is left to their individual children. When the last remaining spouse passes, their entire estate would go to their children. Anything left for their children would be placed into a trust for them and managed for their health, education, maintenance and welfare, with one-half of the principal at 30 and the remaining balance at 35 with asset protection on their inheritance.

**Erik and Sara.** Erik and Sara each have two children from previous relationships. They do not have any children together.

<u>What they did</u>. Erik and Sara each set up their estate plans so that when one passed, their individual estate would be held in a trust for the benefit of their own children. The one exception is that the surviving spouse could remain in the home as long as they wished. Upon the sale of the home, half of the proceeds would go into a trust for the children of the spouse who passed, and half would go the surviving spouse (or to that spouse's children if the second spouse had passed). Anything left for their children would be placed into a trust for them and managed for their health, education, maintenance and welfare, with one-third of the principal at 25, one-third of the principal at 30 and the remaining balance at 35 with asset protection on their inheritance.

**John and Becky.** John and Becky have two minor children together. John also has two college-aged sons from a previous relationship.

<u>What they did</u>. In their estate plans, both John and Becky have decided to treat all the children equally in their planning. That means John's two sons from his previous relationship will receive an equal share of both John's estate and Becky's estate.

How each of you decides who should manage your assets, who should receive what, from whom, and when, is entirely up to you, as long as you have a properly drafted estate plan that takes into account the state laws that apply to blended families. If you do not, a court will decide and your assets could end up going to someone you would not want, and in a manner you would not want.

If you have a blended family, it is important that you find an attorney who has experience in working with blended families, who will take the time to fully explain options to you and make sure that your plan reflects your unique goals and wishes.

# CHAPTER 16

# Instructions For Your Guardians And Caregivers

In the event your guardians were asked to take care of your kids, you would want to make sure they have the information they need. It would be a difficult time for your children as well as for your guardians, and the more information you can give them about your children, their routine, and your family, the easier the transition will be on all of them.

Here are some of the informational items you should put in writing and include in your estate plan for your guardians.

**Instructions Concerning Immediate Family and Friends.** You should make a list of any friends and family members who you would like to be consulted regarding the manner in which your kids will be raised. You should also list friends and family members who are important to you and with whom you want your kids to continue to have a relationship. Unless you provide instructions to your guardians, they may not know this important information.

**Important Information About Each of Your Children.** You should list the full names, date of birth and the location where your children were born. You should list your children's primary physician and secondary physicians, as well as the location of your children's medical records. If any of your kids has a medical condition, make sure you list that, along with any medications and treatments they need.

**Financial.** Take the time to write down, in your own words, your most important priorities for the financial resources you have left for your kids. If you give your children an allowance or plan to do so at a certain age, list out what this is and how it is earned. Let your guardian(s) and your trustee(s) know how you feel about a car when your children are old enough to drive. Would you be in favor of them owning one? Would you be willing to pay for all of it, or only for a portion of it? How much would you be willing to spend? What types of vehicles would you consider and which ones would you rule out for your kids?

Also, take the time to write down, again in your own words, how you would like your guardian to teach your children about the value of money and list out the items you would feel comfortable being purchased for your child. This will make it much easier on your guardian(s) and trustee(s) to know what you would want money spent on as well as what you would not.

**Community.** If you and your kids are involved in community organizations and activities, let your guardians know what those are and whether or not you would like your kids to continue in them. If you have certain charitable organizations that you have been involved with such as Feed My Starving Children or Habitat for Humanity and you would like your kids to either stay involved or get involved when they are old enough, just let your guardian know.

**Values.** Write down the personal values that are most important to you and that you would want your children to be taught. Give your potential guardians instructions as to how you would want them to teach those values to your children.

**Religion and Spirituality.** If you have raised your children in a particular religious tradition and would like that to continue, take the time to write it down and let your guardian know.

**Education.** Do your children attend a public school, a private school or are they home-schooled? Would you like them to continue where they are or would you be comfortable with them moving to a new school and/or school district? If your kids are in a private school and you would like them to remain there, make sure you let your guardian(s) and trustee(s) know that you intend that the money you left for your children be used for them to remain at their private school.

Would you want your guardian to attend all school conferences? How about attending family activities? Volunteering? How would you want report cards discussed and educational success rewarded? Do you want money to be used to help round out your children's educational experience such as paying for band, sports, cultural events, national travel or international travel? Take the time to write down your thoughts and directions for your guardian(s).

**Discipline.** What are your thoughts on discipline? What forms do you believe are acceptable and what forms do you feel are unacceptable to you? Do you have different strategies for each of your kids and, if so, why?

The more direction you can give to your guardians, the easier it will be for them and the easier the transition will be for your kids. Remember, if this is occurring, then something has happened to you and it is going to be an extremely difficult time for your kids. The easier you can make it on them and your guardian(s), the better.

To make this process easier for our clients, we provide them with an instruction form for their guardians that they can complete and include in their estate planning binder.

# CHAPTER 17

# Remember To Revisit Your Plan

When done properly, your estate plan is a reflection of you, your family, your life and your values. However, these can change and often do, particularly when you have kids. In order for your estate plan to reflect your family and your values, it needs to be revisited from time to time to make sure it will continue to work when it is needed.

If any of the following occur, you should revisit and possibly update your estate plan:

**The birth of a child.** If you have another child, you should update your estate plan. In our office, we draft all of our wills and trusts in such a way that additional children are automatically provided for in the plan. That being said, not all plans do. If your will or trust was not drafted so as to provide for additional children, you will want to make sure that your new son or daughter is included. You should also make sure that your short-term guardian paperwork and guardian instructions are updated to include your new son or daughter.

**Federal or state laws affecting your estate plan change.** If there is a change in a state or federal law that would affect your planning, you should have it updated. For example, if your state does not have an estate tax but were to later adopt one, you would want to make sure your planning accommodated that change so as to provide for your children instead of the government. If your state has an estate tax but changes the size of the estates it impacts, you would also want to make sure your planning accommodates that change. If your state were to adopt new statutes on the naming of guardians, you will want to make sure your planning is up to date.

**The size of your estate changes.** If your estate were to get larger or smaller, you would want to revisit your plan to make sure the planning you have done still fits your circumstances. I can't tell you how many estate plans I have seen over the last few years that required cumbersome and expensive accounting and asset allocations after the death of a spouse because the plans were never updated to reflect changes in the size of the estate and the laws. I have also seen many families pay large amounts in federal and state estate taxes because they did not update their plans to reflect changes in the size of their estate and the law. If either the size of your estate or the estate tax exemptions change, you should make an appointment to have your plan reviewed by a competent attorney.

**A guardian, personal representative or trustee is no longer able to serve.** If you have named someone to act as a short- or long-term guardian of your children as a personal representative or trustee, and they are no longer able to serve for whatever reason, you need to have your plan updated. If you do not, you run the risk of leaving those important decisions up to a judge.

**You wish to change who your guardian, personal representative or trustee is.** If you no longer wish to have your appointed guardian(s), personal representative or trustee serve, then you will need to make those changes.

**The death of a spouse.** If you should lose your spouse, you will want to have your plan reviewed. Your spouse is often named as your personal representative, trustee, agent in your financial power of attorney and/or agent in your health care directive. You will need to make sure you have alternates named to act.

**Divorce.** If you and your spouse were to divorce, you will need to update your plan. It is highly likely that your soon-to-be ex-spouse is named in some capacity in your plan – often as a personal representative, trustee, executor and/or power of attorney. Many people neglect to revisit their plans after their divorce, often believing that the divorce settlement changes their planning. It often doesn't. You will also want to make sure that you update beneficiary designations on retirement accounts, life insurance, checking, savings and brokerage accounts.

Several recent cases throughout the U.S. illustrate what can happen if you fail to update your plan after a divorce. In one of the more high profile cases, a man passed away leaving his entire estate to his wife. However, he did not change the beneficiary of his life insurance policy from his ex-wife to his new wife. The ex-wife sought to keep the proceeds from the policy while the new wife fought to keep the proceeds as part of the estate. The case made it all the way to the U.S. Supreme Court – which sided with the ex-wife.

**Your children reach adulthood.** Once your children reach adulthood, you may decide to name them as your personal representative(s), trustee(s), agent(s) for your financial affairs and/or agent(s) for your health care decisions.

I once had a young woman and her brother who were referred to me for help after the passing of their father. Their dad's will named his sister, the children's aunt, to be his personal representative. He had done this when the children were very young and when he and his children were close to their aunt.

Years after the will was finalized, the father, the young woman, and her brother had a falling-out with their aunt and had not spoken since. The father passed when the children were in their late twenties, ready and able to take on the role as personal representative. Unfortunately, since the will had not been updated since the discord with the aunt, she was still named as the personal representative in the will. The aunt saw this as an opportunity to take another jab at the children over the falling-out that had occurred years earlier. She refused to relinquish her role and would not allow the children to step in and deal with their father's estate themselves. Unfortunately, this also meant that the aunt would receive thousands of dollars in fees as the personal representative that would otherwise have gone to the children.

Despite the odds, we attempted to replace the aunt as personal representative with the children. The judge refused, noting that their father could have changed his will at any time to replace the aunt with his children and that he, the judge, would not replace the judgment of the father with his own. It was the correct decision under the law, but an unfortunate result for the kids.

**You move to another state.** If you move to another state, you should have your plan reviewed to make sure it will work under the laws of your new home. For example, if your plan was drafted to deal with the estate tax in your previous state of residence but your current state has either a different estate tax exemption amount or no estate tax at all, you will want to make sure your plan reflects those changes. Some states also have specific statutes for how to name short-term guardians while other states have no current laws in place, so you will want to make sure that your short-term guardianship paperwork is updated, if necessary, and will work in your new state.

**Your causes and charities change.** If charitable giving was drafted into your estate plan and the causes and charities you participate in have changed, make sure those changes are reflected in your planning.

**You wish to change your beneficiaries.** If, for some reason, you would like to change who will receive your estate upon your passing, you will need to make those changes to your estate plan. This can be particularly important if one of your children develops a disability. If you fail to change your plan to reflect this, anything your child inherits could cause them to lose government benefits. You should instead update your plan to include a supplemental needs trust for your child. For more information on supplemental needs trusts, see Chapter 14.

**If it has been more than three years since your plan has been reviewed.** Everyone should have their plan reviewed by a competent attorney at least every five years to make sure it is up-to-date with current laws. That being said, I advise all of my clients with minor children to have their plans reviewed every three years at the latest. As parents of minor children, our lives and our families are changing more frequently and we need to track those changes more closely. For example, you may find that the guardians who are appropriate for your kids when they are toddlers may not fit as well when they are teenagers.

Just recently, a mom shared the following story with me at an event where I spoke. She and her husband had completed their estate plans several years earlier. As a trip was approaching, she had a "niggling sense" that she needed to have her plan reviewed "before we boarded the plane". She did not have any updates in mind; she was responding more to a gut feeling. When she brought her plan in to be reviewed, she realized that the family members they had named when they first completed their plan had since developed substance abuse issues. As she said, "Had we not updated our plan and had something happened to us, we would have put our children and our life savings into the hands of dysfunctional people."

An estate plan is not meant to be stored away and forgotten. It should be a reflection of your current situation, so it is important to have your estate plan reviewed at least every five years to make sure it will work as planned when it is needed.

# CHAPTER 18

# Preserving And Passing On Family Heirlooms

Family heirlooms are often some of the most treasured pieces of an inheritance. An old silk pocket square may not be worth much, but it takes on a whole new meaning and value when you discover that it was a gift from your great-grandmother to your great-grandfather on their wedding day. A family photo album becomes a true treasure when the people in the photos are identified and the story or stories surrounding the photo are catalogued and passed on. The tea set on your shelf may not have a lot of value to anyone else, but to you it is a treasure, a valued memory of having tea with your grandmother on Sunday mornings.

Another story may help illustrate the importance of this. The summer after my grandparents passed away, my uncle was visiting from Colorado. While sitting around my parents' dining room table one evening, he mentioned that he got Grandma's mixing bowl and wooden mixing spoon. My grandmother had an old bowl and spoon that she got from her mother and we think might have belonged to my great, great grandmother. My grandmother always had this bowl and spoon in the center of the table at the holidays. My uncle then shared that every time he sees this mixing bowl and spoon he can't help but tear up, because they bring back vivid memories of special holidays shared with my grandma. He said, "These are nickel items, at best, at a garage sale. They have no value or meaning to anyone else, but they mean the world to me."

My brother has already asked for my dad's cap in advance, his favorite one that he has worn for years. Of all the things my parents have, the one thing my brother really wants is a simple black cap, an item that could be purchased for a couple of bucks at any store, but that has special meaning to him.

I was fortunate enough to inherit my grandfather's rocking chair. I feel close to him whenever I sit in it. I keep it in my home office and frequently sit in it while I read or work. In fact, I wrote this entire book while sitting in it.

Unfortunately, more family disputes also arise over family heirlooms, photos, jewelry and other personal property than over money. That is why it is so important to include a written list with your estate plan of who should receive these items and, particularly if you have minor children, when they should receive them.

Many attorneys advocate listing specific gifts in your will or trust. However, if the laws in your state allow it, I suggest that you not make those gifts inside the body of your will or trust, but rather on a separate signed document that is mentioned in the body of your estate plan. That way, if you ever change your mind about your list, you can simply prepare a new one. If you put these gifts in the main body of your will or trust, then you will need to amend your will or trust if you ever change your mind. Also, by creating a separate list you can complete your will or trust and then add the list at a later date if you'd like a little extra time to put the list together. You should seek the advice of a competent attorney to determine the requirements your state may have for the preparation of a list like this.

The time you take to catalog family heirlooms and list who should get them and when will go a long way toward keeping family traditions alive and maintaining peace in your family.

# CHAPTER 19

# Legacy Planning: How To Provide A Lifetime Of Love & Guidance To Your Children In The Event You Aren't There For Them

I've saved this section for the end of the book because up until now, everything else that was discussed has a government default plan in place for dealing with it. As noted throughout the book, if you don't get a written plan in place there is a process for dealing with your stuff and determining who should raise your children. You may not like it. It may not be what you would have wanted. It may even be overly time-consuming and expensive, but there is a process in place for taking care of it. However, there is one set of assets that only you can capture and pass on, and these may be the most important and valuable assets you have to give to your children.

Your wealth includes more than just your money or your things. In fact, your money and belongings are only a small portion of your total wealth, particularly as a parent. Your total wealth includes your emotional, intellectual and spiritual assets; it includes your values and goals, your stories and experiences, and it may be far more valuable, especially to your children and grandchildren, than your material possessions. As your children grow, you share and pass these on to them naturally. However, what happens if something happens to you and you aren't there to share these with them? How do you make sure that you capture this particularly valuable portion of your wealth, and make sure it gets passed along to your children?

These questions took on new meaning to me when I was forced to face them head-on. At the ripe old age of 31, my doctor stood at the end of my hospital bed and told me I had 48 hours or less to get my affairs in order. Here I was, a former member of the college crew team who still ate right and was in great physical shape, being told I had 48 hours to live.

It all had started with a bad cold over the holidays that had improved by New Year's. Then, one day I woke up with a rash on my legs and a metallic taste in my mouth. My in-laws were in town for a visit, so I showed the rash to my father-in-law, who is a physician. He said it appeared to be petichiae and suggested I go in to urgent care and get it checked out.

When I arrived at the clinic, the doctor pricked the tip of my right index finger, collected some blood in a test tube and headed off to the lab for some tests. I noticed that blood was soaking through the cotton ball and that whenever I let up on the pressure, it dripped out of my fingertip like a leaky faucet. I knew something was not right even before the doctor returned. When she did, her face was as white as her lab coat and she told me to get to the emergency room immediately. At the hospital, I was informed that my platelet levels were dangerously low. Doctors treated my condition aggressively, but the treatments did not work and my platelet count was still at dangerous levels.

Two days later, my doctor stood at the foot of my bed and told me they had done everything they could do and that I now had 48 hours or less to get my affairs in order. Apparently, the virus that caused my cold over the holidays contained a protein that was similar enough to a protein marker on my platelets that my immune system didn't know the difference. My immune system was now destroying my platelets and every solution the doctors attempted had failed. The official medical diagnosis was idiopathic thrombocytopenia purpura (ITP).

A few hours after I was given the prognosis, my wife, daughter and I were talking together in my room. My daughter Katie was just two months shy of her third birthday. As long as I live, I will never forget her earnest blue eyes as she locked onto mine and asked me, "Daddy, when are you coming home?" My heart broke. I didn't know what to tell her. I didn't know how to tell her. So, I simply answered, "Daddy is pretty sick honey. I'm not sure when I'll come home."

That evening, I reflected on what I was leaving for my wife and daughter. I had a life insurance policy in place to financially care for my wife and daughter. My wife is a fantastic mom and I knew she would get the help and support she needed from her parents and mine. However, all I had left my daughter was a scrapbook full of photos and a sizeable life insurance policy. I wondered if she would even remember me. If she did, what would she remember?

I thought of all the things I would miss: her first day of kindergarten, dance recitals, her 16th birthday, her graduation from high school, college, her wedding, becoming a mom. I thought about all the things I wanted to tell her as she reached those milestones in life. I thought of all the things I wanted to tell her about her great-grandparents. About how two of her great-grandfathers had served in World War II and then returned home to rural Minnesota, settled down and became farmers and raised families. How I used to sit with my grandfather and talk about history outside behind the house, or about how we spent long, lazy summer afternoons fishing together and then came home and cleaned fish while my grandma dipped them in beer batter and fried them up.

I wanted to tell her about summers spent mowing lawns and going to the local A&W for root beer and hamburgers with my grandparents. I wanted to tell her about going ice fishing with my dad and his buddies as a boy and getting to have a sip of Dad's beer with the admonition, "don't tell Mom." (I would find out years later that Mom already knew). I wanted to share with her stories of the fun adventures my brothers and I had when we were young. As I thought about all of this, I realized that I had not captured and passed along to her who I was and how much I loved her. Despite doing everything a smart attorney does, I realized that there was more I could have done.

When I walked out of the hospital 72 hours later – my doctors called me a walking miracle – I set out to fix my oversights. I began recording things for my daughter. If this ever happened again, I wanted to be able to share my love, guidance and values with her. Then the light bulb went off . . .

In our practice, when we have completed an estate plan for our clients we offer to record a legacy video for them. We have a library of topics that our clients can choose from. Once they have chosen a topic or two, we guide them through a series of questions related to that topic and capture their message on video. We include a DVD of their interview as part of their estate plan. The topics vary, but can include a message of love, what you find special about each of your kids, instructions to guardians and trustees, or an explanation of what you've done in your planning and why. The important thing is to capture your most valuable assets of all, your love, guidance and experiences, and pass them on to your children.

If something were to happen to you, some of the most valuable assets you have, particularly if you have small children, are your emotional, spiritual, and intellectual assets: your love, guidance, and family traditions. Make sure you capture those assets and pass them along to your children and grandchildren.

If ever you aren't able to be there for your children, they would love being able to put in a DVD and see your smile and hear you, in your own voice, tell them that you love them. Your love and support may be the most important and most valuable things you can leave for them.

# ILIT

Irrovocable Life Insurance trust
- Keep life insurance proceeds out of taxable
  limits
-

Revocable
A Living Trust is a treasure chest that we
can place and title our assets to avoid probate


## Beneficiary Dynasty Trust


WA